Practicing Presence™ with Inner Kindness

A 31-Day Mindfulness Journal

Practicing Presence™ with Inner Kindness

A 31-Day Mindfulness Journal

dLee

EssenceOfAuthenticPresence.com

© 2020 Mighty Spectrums LLC, U.S.A. All Rights Reserved
ISBN: 978-0-578-60169-4

FORWARD

What is *Practicing Presence™ with Inner Kindness*?

Presence can be described as an act of "being" in the moment.... synonymous with mindfulness. Practicing presence is the intentional activity of quietly focusing ones attention on the present moment, in a relaxed manner and without judgment. When coupled with inner kindness, practicing presence becomes a ritual of self-care that is not only relaxing, but is also highly beneficial. The benefits for engaging in kindness and for practicing presence are startlingly similar: both activities lower stress, increase positive feelings of satisfaction and joy, and deepen feelings of relaxation. In addition, both mindfulness and kindness have been demonstrated to decrease feelings of anxiety and depression, while increasing positive feelings of connection to other people, and to life in general.

Most of us have been conditioned to believe that being active and productive, engaged in multiple activities, and leading busy lives are all signs of a good life that is well lived. It is easy for us to become so active in our everyday lives that we sometimes lose sight of the present moment. Our lives, and the lives of our children have become so structured and filled with activities that time has become a precious commodity, and we often feel overwhelmed. The cost of this "good" life is often increased stress, lower productivity, insomnia, and internal dissatisfaction which may show up as addictions, emotional or physical imbalances, and low self-esteem.

What if there is an antidote to this modern-day dilemma? What if there's a way to slow things down? What if there is a way to find more meaning in every day moments? What if we learn to take care of ourselves in such a way that we experience greater satisfaction in our every day lives, while increasing joy and happiness?

Practicing Presence™ with Inner Kindness is a beautiful and simple method for engaging in daily acts of kindness through mindfulness-based activities. As these activities are practiced through-out the month, old patterns of thought and behavior start to loosen and one becomes more attuned to the present moment.

Recommendations for using this book:
- Set aside time each day to reflect and write in your book. This is your sacred time. Treat this time as important and do not allow anything to interrupt you. Let others in your household know this is your time, and not to disturb you for at least 20 minutes.
- Create a daily ritual for yourself: make a cup of tea or coffee, light a candle, turn off your cell phone, get comfy.
- Write with authenticity and acceptance. Allow whatever wants to be expressed to come out. Let go of judgment.
- EnJOY yourself. This is a beautiful time with yourself; I promise if you give yourself this gift, you will be very glad you did.

It has been my pleasure and honor to witness the unfolding of this lovely book and process. dLee's intentions come from the purest place of wanting to offer a gift to the world that will allow others to engage more meaningfully in life through the practice of presence.

May your journey into this work be deeply meaningful and rewarding.

Namaste,

Alesia Regan-Hughes
Intuitive Reiki Master, Namaste Healing Arts

https://www.massagebook.com/Kirkland~Massage~namaste-healing-arts
Founder of Be Kind to Everyone Day, August 28th
https://www.facebook.com/bekindtoeveryoneday/

Life is not measured by the number of breaths we take
but by the moments that take our breath away.
~ Author Unknown

8

Introduction

How do the following two phrases make you feel?

1. *"I am no good at anything and no one loves me."*
    These words can make you feel heavy and slow.

2. *"Yeah! I have successfully made it through a very hectic week with help from a lot of people around me."*
    These words can feel uplifting and express gratitude for the assistance.

Thoughts and images from your inner dialogue affect the choice of words you express verbally to yourself and others. These word choices directly affect the vibrational frequency you experience in your outer world and how you generally feel about life.

J Loren Norris said, *"It takes a new way of thinking, speaking and acting. It takes a change in habits, and a better understanding of who you are and what you do each day. It takes a foolproof formula you can apply to every minute of your day, for the most excellent outcome every time."*

When you make improvements to your personal way of talking to yourself, the effect can be dramatic. You can start taking steps from wherever you are:
    Step 1 - Become aware of your thought patterns.
    Step 2 - Catch the negative verbal patterns in action and immediately replace them with optimistic, high-energy words.
    Step 3 - Nurture yourself with supportive thoughts, word choices and uplifting images.
    Step 4 - Practice presence with full conscious effort.

It has been said it takes 31 days of practicing something to create a new habit. Have patience and compassion for yourself as you discover a new way of being. No matter how small the changes seem in the moment, watch how new blossoms of inner kindness and mindfulness show up in your outside world.

I can do this!

How to use Your Practicing Presence Journal

This is Your Journey - give yourself patience as you practice being present. With time, space and reflection, it will become your chosen way of being.

Kindness is an inner desire that makes us want to do good things even if we do not get anything in return. It is the joy of our life to do them. When we do good things from this inner desire, there is kindness in everything we think, say, want and do. ~ Emanuel Swedenborg

How to embrace this mindful practice using all of your senses

1. Pick a time of day when you are alert and can be undisturbed.

2. Find a cozy spot where you can focus.

3. Clear your mind. Let thoughts come in but allow them to leave.

4. Reflect on your day and how each sense was present for you.

5. Add color to any pages if you feel inspired.

6. Make journal notes along the way during your day.

7. Track your activities that support your mind, body and spirit.

8. How do you feel?

**Your First Baby Picture
As a Bud Beginning to Open
(Place photo here or draw your own)**

Your understanding of your inner self holds the meaning of your life.
~ Leo Tolstoy

How to Immerse Yourself

Pause and step into each photo scene
It welcomes you with openness as it simply is
Breathe in and hold the image in your internal mind screen
You have the front row seat
In your unfolding experience and mindful beat
Breath out and let anything go that is not your desired being.
~ dLee

Optimistic, High-Energy Words to Use

Abundant	Enterprising	Imaginative	Precious	Start
Achieve	Enthusiastic	Impact	Prepared	Stimulate
Act	Excellent	Industrious	Present	Strong
Active	Excite	Innovative	Productive	Stunning
Aligned	Experienced	Inspire	Propose	Success
Appreciate	Exquisite	Intuitive	Qualified	Superb
Authentic	Fabulous	Inventive	Quick	Surprise
Beautiful	Far-sighted	Joyous	Radiant	Taught
Believe	Fascinating	Kind	Reasonable	Tenacious
Boost	Feel	Lift	Refreshing	Thankful
Bright	Flourishing	Limitless	Relaxing	Thriving
Build	Focus	Luminous	Release	Timely
Buoyant	Fortunate	Link	Reliable	Track
Calm	Free	Love	Resourceful	Train
Capable	Fulfilled	Magical	Respected	Trusting
Cheerful	Fun	Masterful	Results	Truthful
Connect	Generous	Miraculous	Respond	Unique
Conscious	Genuine	Motivate	Robust	Unite
Considerate	Gifted	Natural	Satisfied	Valuable
Craft	Glorious	Nurturing	Secure	Versatile
Creative	Go	Noble	Self-Reliant	Vibrant
Delicious	Graceful	Optimistic	Sensational	Victorious
Delight	Gracious	Organize	Sensible	Vigorous
Design	Great	Outstanding	Serene	Vivacious
Diligent	Guide	Passionate	Shape	Vivid
Dream	Happy	Peaceful	Show	Well
Dynamic	Harmony	Persevering	Smart	Whole
Efficient	Heart	Persistent	Sparkling	Wise
Elegant	Helpful	Plan	Spectacular	Wonder
Eloquent	Honest	Plentiful	Spiritual	Zeal
Engaging	Humor	Positive	Splendid	Zest

What you seek is seeking you.
~ Rumi

The Universe doesn't give you what you ask for with your thoughts - it gives you what you demand with your actions.
~ Steve Maraboli

Listen

Take time to really hear
Your streaming internal dialogue
Seemingly so clearly near.
It likely brings up active fears.
Confirm the value is really there
Or just let the words pass on through.
Set a goal to listen and learn
Get a pure focus
Without distractions
Ask yourself open engaging questions
What about the details
Set aside time for silence to really listen
Pay attention to how your body feels
Wrap up the inside summary
With uplifting high-energy words
Practice this on the inside
Then let it out into your world.
~ dLee

POWER WORD SCRAMBLE

CPEERATIAP	
EEAMOSW	
ILSBS	
YUBATON	
RCLUEFEH	
ONCIOCSSU	
EECTORDINSA	
IIEOUDLSC	
GIEIDLTN	
TSLROEESFF	
TOENEQUL	
RITRNESEEP	

SEE PAGE 124 FOR KEY

Practicing Presence™ Day 1

Today I practiced being aware of my thought patterns:
___
___
___

Today I practiced identifying the patterns (beliefs) that get in my way:
___
___
___

Today I practiced planting the following positive seeds of thought:
___
___
___

Today I practiced nurturing and supporting myself by:
___
___
___

Today I practiced consciously allowing myself to pause and feel:
___
___
___

Today I focused on power words and images which resulted in:
___
___
___
___

Notes

Minds are like flowers; they open only when the time is right.
~ Stephen Richards

Don't judge each day by the harvest
you reap but by the seeds you plant.
~ Robert Louis Stevenson

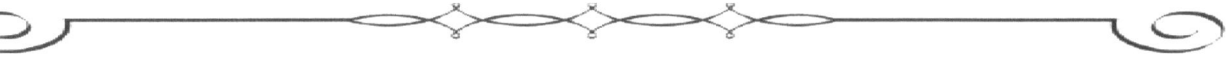

Practicing Presence™ Day 2

Today I practiced being aware of my thought patterns:
_____
_____
_____

Today I practiced identifying the patterns (beliefs) that get in my way:
_____
_____
_____

Today I practiced planting the following positive seeds of thought:
_____
_____
_____

Today I practiced nurturing and supporting myself by:
_____
_____
_____

Today I practiced consciously allowing myself to pause and feel:
_____
_____
_____

Today I focused on power words and images which resulted in:
_____
_____
_____
_____

This is my simple religion. No need for temples. No need for complicated philosogy. Your own mind, your own heart is the temple. Your philosophy is simple kindness...
~ Dalai Lama

Practicing Presence™ Day 3

Today I practiced being aware of my thought patterns:
___
___
___

Today I practiced identifying the patterns (beliefs) that get in my way:
___
___
___

Today I practiced planting the following positive seeds of thought:
___
___
___

Today I practiced nurturing and supporting myself by:
___
___
___

Today I practiced consciously allowing myself to pause and feel:
___
___
___

Today I focused on power words and images which resulted in:
___
___
___
___

Notes

One person's weed is another person's wildflower.
~ Susan Wittig Albert

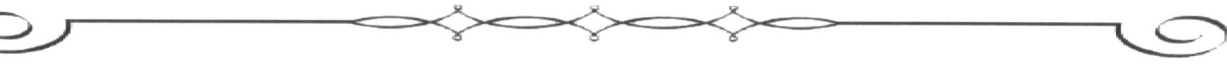

Practicing Presence™ Day 4

Today I practiced being aware of my thought patterns:
___
___
___

Today I practiced identifying the patterns (beliefs) that get in my way:
___
___
___

Today I practiced planting the following positive seeds of thought:
___
___
___

Today I practiced nurturing and supporting myself by:
___
___
___

Today I practiced consciously allowing myself to pause and feel:
___
___
___

Today I focused on power words and images which resulted in:
___
___
___
___

Notes

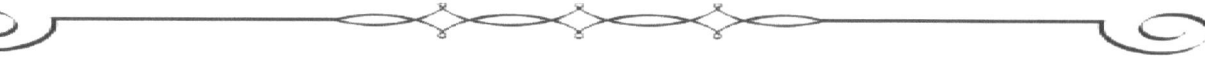

Practicing Presence™ Day 5

Today I practiced being aware of my thought patterns:
_____
_____
_____

Today I practiced identifying the patterns (beliefs) that get in my way:
_____
_____
_____

Today I practiced planting the following positive seeds of thought:
_____
_____
_____

Today I practiced nurturing and supporting myself by:
_____
_____
_____

Today I practiced consciously allowing myself to pause and feel:
_____
_____
_____

Today I focused on power words and images which resulted in:
_____
_____
_____
_____

Notes

Language is the blood of the soul into which thoughts run and out of which they grow.
~ Oliver Wendell Holmes

Mindfulness isn't difficult, we just need to remember to do it.
~ Sharon Salzberg

Practicing Presence™ Day 6

Today I practiced being aware of my thought patterns:
___

Today I practiced identifying the patterns (beliefs) that get in my way:
___

Today I practiced planting the following positive seeds of thought:
___

Today I practiced nurturing and supporting myself by:
___

Today I practiced consciously allowing myself to pause and feel:
___

Today I focused on power words and images which resulted in:
___

Notes

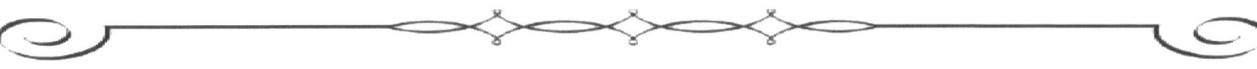

Practicing Presence™ Day 7

Today I practiced being aware of my thought patterns:
___
___

Today I practiced identifying the patterns (beliefs) that get in my way:
___
___

Today I practiced planting the following positive seeds of thought:
___
___

Today I practiced nurturing and supporting myself by:
___
___

Today I practiced consciously allowing myself to pause and feel:
___
___

Today I focused on power words and images which resulted in:
___
___
___

The trouble is you think you have time.
~ Buddha

Notes

If you become a helper of hearts,
springs of wisdom will flow from your heart.
~ Rumi

Always hold fast to the present. Every situation, indeed every moment, is of infinite value, for it is the representative of a whole eternity.
~ Johann Wolfgang von Goethe

Practicing Presence™ Day 8

Today I practiced being aware of my thought patterns:
___
___
___

Today I practiced identifying the patterns (beliefs) that get in my way:
___
___
___

Today I practiced planting the following positive seeds of thought:
___
___
___

Today I practiced nurturing and supporting myself by:
___
___
___

Today I practiced consciously allowing myself to pause and feel:
___
___
___

Today I focused on power words and images which resulted in:
___
___
___
___

Notes

Plant seeds of happiness, hope, success, and love; it will all come back to you in abundance. This is the law of nature.
~ Steve Maraboli

Practicing Presence™ Day 9

Today I practiced being aware of my thought patterns:
___
___
___

Today I practiced identifying the patterns (beliefs) that get in my way:
___
___
___

Today I practiced planting the following positive seeds of thought:
___
___
___

Today I practiced nurturing and supporting myself by:
___
___
___

Today I practiced consciously allowing myself to pause and feel:
___
___
___

Today I focused on power words and images which resulted in:
___
___
___
___

Notes

A seed grows with no sound but a tree falls with huge noise. Destruction has noise, but creation is quiet. This is the power of silence... Grow silently.
~ Author Unknown

Practicing Presence™ Day 10

Today I practiced being aware of my thought patterns:
___
___
___

Today I practiced identifying the patterns (beliefs) that get in my way:
___
___
___

Today I practiced planting the following positive seeds of thought:
___
___
___

Today I practiced nurturing and supporting myself by:
___
___
___

Today I practiced consciously allowing myself to pause and feel:
___
___
___

Today I focused on power words and images which resulted in:
___
___
___
___

The leaves and the light are one.
~ Albert Einstein

Practicing Presence™ Day 11

Today I practiced being aware of my thought patterns:
___
___
___

Today I practiced identifying the patterns (beliefs) that get in my way:
___
___
___

Today I practiced planting the following positive seeds of thought:
___
___
___

Today I practiced nurturing and supporting myself by:
___
___
___

Today I practiced consciously allowing myself to pause and feel:
___
___
___

Today I focused on power words and images which resulted in:
___
___
___
___

Never discourage anyone who continually makes progress,
no matter how slow.
~ Plato

Practicing Presence™ Day 12

Today I practiced being aware of my thought patterns:
_____
_____

Today I practiced identifying the patterns (beliefs) that get in my way:
_____
_____

Today I practiced planting the following positive seeds of thought:
_____
_____

Today I practiced nurturing and supporting myself by:
_____
_____

Today I practiced consciously allowing myself to pause and feel:
_____
_____

Today I focused on power words and images which resulted in:
_____
_____
_____

Notes

Dragonflies are reminders that we are light and we can reflect light in powerful ways if we choose to do so.
~ Robyn Nola

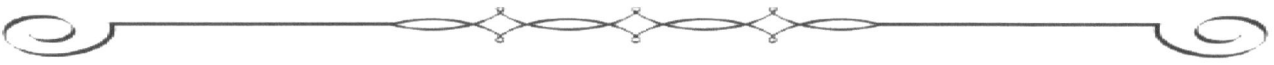

Practicing Presence™ Day 13

Today I practiced being aware of my thought patterns:
___
___
___

Today I practiced identifying the patterns (beliefs) that get in my way:
___
___
___

Today I practiced planting the following positive seeds of thought:
___
___
___

Today I practiced nurturing and supporting myself by:
___
___
___

Today I practiced consciously allowing myself to pause and feel:
___
___
___

Today I focused on power words and images which resulted in:
___
___
___
___

Mindfulness is the aware, balanced acceptance of the present experience. It isn't more complicated than that. It is opening to or receiving the present moment, pleasant or unpleasant, just as it is, without either clinging to it or rejecting it.
~ Sylvia Boorstein

Practicing Presence™ Day 14

Today I practiced being aware of my thought patterns:
___
___

Today I practiced identifying the patterns (beliefs) that get in my way:
___
___

Today I practiced planting the following positive seeds of thought:
___
___

Today I practiced nurturing and supporting myself by:
___
___

Today I practiced consciously allowing myself to pause and feel:
___
___

Today I focused on power words and images which resulted in:
___
___
___
___

HIGH ENERGY WORD SEARCH

G	M	O	P	T	I	M	I	S	T	I	C
W	Y	N	O	M	R	A	H	N	K	U	K
S	P	A	R	K	L	I	N	G	Q	C	J
P	N	I	X	G	N	O	R	T	S	G	K
H	T	T	T	H	A	N	K	F	U	L	A
A	N	H	S	U	O	I	C	I	L	E	D
P	A	R	T	L	U	F	E	C	A	R	G
K	I	I	Z	H	R	E	D	N	O	W	W
V	D	V	H	L	F	A	E	X	E	C	K
M	A	I	N	T	N	A	D	N	U	B	A
S	R	N	B	E	A	U	T	I	F	U	L
M	U	G	J	W	X	L	O	Y	F	G	X

SEE PAGE 124 FOR KEY

ABUNDANT
THANKFUL
SPARKLING
GRACEFUL

WONDER
THRIVING
DELICIOUS
HARMONY

STRONG
RADIANT
BEAUTIFUL
OPTIMISTIC

No person, no place, and no thing has any
power over us, for 'we' are the only thinkers
in our minds. When we create peace and
harmony and balance in our minds,
we will find it in our lives.
~ Louise L. Hay

Love springs from the inside. It is the immortal surge of passion, excitement, energy, power, strength, prosperity, recognition, respect, desire, determination, enthusiasm, confidence, courage, and vitality, that nourishes, extends and protects. It possesses an external objective - life.
~ Ogwo David Emenike

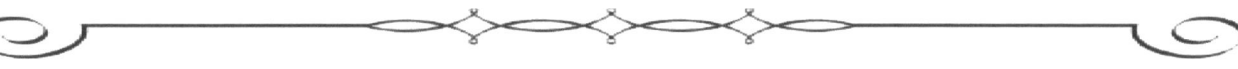

Practicing Presence™ Day 15

Today I practiced being aware of my thought patterns:
_____
_____
_____

Today I practiced identifying the patterns (beliefs) that get in my way:
_____
_____
_____

Today I practiced planting the following positive seeds of thought:
_____
_____
_____

Today I practiced nurturing and supporting myself by:
_____
_____
_____

Today I practiced consciously allowing myself to pause and feel:
_____
_____
_____

Today I focused on power words and images which resulted in:
_____
_____
_____
_____

Notes

When you have confidence, you can have a lot of fun. And when you have fun, you can do amazing things.
~ Joe Namath

Notes

The more you extend kindness to yourself, the more it will become your automatic response to others...
~ Wayne Dyer

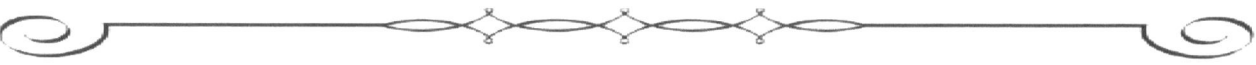

Practicing Presence™ Day 16

Today I practiced being aware of my thought patterns:
_____
_____
_____

Today I practiced identifying the patterns (beliefs) that get in my way:
_____
_____
_____

Today I practiced planting the following positive seeds of thought:
_____
_____
_____

Today I practiced nurturing and supporting myself by:
_____
_____
_____

Today I practiced consciously allowing myself to pause and feel:
_____
_____
_____

Today I focused on power words and images which resulted in:
_____
_____
_____
_____

Practicing Presence™ Day 17

Today I practiced being aware of my thought patterns:
_____
_____
_____

Today I practiced identifying the patterns (beliefs) that get in my way:
_____
_____
_____

Today I practiced planting the following positive seeds of thought:
_____
_____
_____

Today I practiced nurturing and supporting myself by:
_____
_____
_____

Today I practiced consciously allowing myself to pause and feel:
_____
_____
_____

Today I focused on power words and images which resulted in:
_____
_____
_____
_____

Just let go - and fall like a little waterfall.
~ Bob Ross

Notes

The golden opportunity you are seeking is in yourself. It is not in your environment, it is not in luck or chance, or the help of others; it is in yourself alone.
~ Orison Swett Marden

Practicing Presence™ Day 18

Today I practiced being aware of my thought patterns:
___
___
___

Today I practiced identifying the patterns (beliefs) that get in my way:
___
___
___

Today I practiced planting the following positive seeds of thought:
___
___
___

Today I practiced nurturing and supporting myself by:
___
___
___

Today I practiced consciously allowing myself to pause and feel:
___
___
___

Today I focused on power words and images which resulted in:
___
___
___
___

Practicing Presence™ Day 19

Today I practiced being aware of my thought patterns:
_____
_____
_____

Today I practiced identifying the patterns (beliefs) that get in my way:
_____
_____
_____

Today I practiced planting the following positive seeds of thought:
_____
_____
_____

Today I practiced nurturing and supporting myself by:
_____
_____
_____

Today I practiced consciously allowing myself to pause and feel:
_____
_____
_____

Today I focused on power words and images which resulted in:
_____
_____
_____
_____

The softest things in the world overcome the hardest things in the world.
~ Lao Tzu

Notes

Respond; don't react.
Listen; don't talk.
Think; don't assume.
～ Raji Lukkoor

Practicing Presence™ Day 20

Today I practiced being aware of my thought patterns:
_____
_____

Today I practiced identifying the patterns (beliefs) that get in my way:
_____
_____

Today I practiced planting the following positive seeds of thought:
_____
_____

Today I practiced nurturing and supporting myself by:
_____
_____

Today I practiced consciously allowing myself to pause and feel:
_____
_____

Today I focused on power words and images which resulted in:
_____
_____
_____
_____

Notes

We never seem to have enough time to take care of ourselves in our chaotic lives. Take the approach that you are worth treating yourself to a unique and beautiful bouquet... just because.
~ dLee

Practicing Presence™ Day 21

Today I practiced being aware of my thought patterns:
___
___

Today I practiced identifying the patterns (beliefs) that get in my way:
___
___

Today I practiced planting the following positive seeds of thought:
___
___

Today I practiced nurturing and supporting myself by:
___
___

Today I practiced consciously allowing myself to pause and feel:
___
___

Today I focused on power words and images which resulted in:
___
___
___
___

When you take a flower in your hand and
really look at it, it's your world for a moment.
~ Georgia O'Keeffe

In this moment, there is plenty of time. In this moment, you are precisely as you should be.
In this moment, there is infinite possibility.
~ Victoria Moran

Practicing Presence™ Day 22

Today I practiced being aware of my thought patterns:
___
___
___

Today I practiced identifying the patterns (beliefs) that get in my way:
___
___
___

Today I practiced planting the following positive seeds of thought:
___
___
___

Today I practiced nurturing and supporting myself by:
___
___
___

Today I practiced consciously allowing myself to pause and feel:
___
___
___

Today I focused on power words and images which resulted in:
___
___
___
___

Notes

Trees have spirit... just talk to them, reach out
and connect with them.
~ dLee

Notes

Practicing Presence™ Day 23

Today I practiced being aware of my thought patterns:
___
___
___

Today I practiced identifying the patterns (beliefs) that get in my way:
___
___
___

Today I practiced planting the following positive seeds of thought:
___
___
___

Today I practiced nurturing and supporting myself by:
___
___
___

Today I practiced consciously allowing myself to pause and feel:
___
___
___

Today I focused on power words and images which resulted in:
___
___
___
___

The practice of mindfulness begins in the small, remote cave of your unconscious mind and blossoms with the sunlight of your conscious life, reaching far beyond the people and places you can see.
~ Earon Davis

Practicing Presence™ Day 24

Today I practiced being aware of my thought patterns:
___
___
___

Today I practiced identifying the patterns (beliefs) that get in my way:
___
___
___

Today I practiced planting the following positive seeds of thought:
___
___
___

Today I practiced nurturing and supporting myself by:
___
___
___

Today I practiced consciously allowing myself to pause and feel:
___
___
___

Today I focused on power words and images which resulted in:
___
___
___
___

Notes

Unexpected kindness is the most powerful, least costly, and most underrated agent of human change.
~ Bob Kerrey

Notes

Practicing Presence™ Day 25

Today I practiced being aware of my thought patterns:
___
___
___

Today I practiced identifying the patterns (beliefs) that get in my way:
___
___
___

Today I practiced planting the following positive seeds of thought:
___
___
___

Today I practiced nurturing and supporting myself by:
___
___
___

Today I practiced consciously allowing myself to pause and feel:
___
___
___

Today I focused on power words and images which resulted in:
___
___
___
___

By breaking down our sense of self-importance, all
we lose is a parasite that has long infected our minds.
What we gain in return is freedom, openness of
mind, spontaneity, simplicity, altruism:
all qualities inherent in happiness.
~ Matthieu Ricard

Practicing Presence™ Day 26

Today I practiced being aware of my thought patterns:
___
___

Today I practiced identifying the patterns (beliefs) that get in my way:
___
___

Today I practiced planting the following positive seeds of thought:
___
___

Today I practiced nurturing and supporting myself by:
___
___

Today I practiced consciously allowing myself to pause and feel:
___
___

Today I focused on power words and images which resulted in:
___
___
___
___

Notes

In a gentle way, you can shake the world.
~ Mahatma Gandhi

Notes

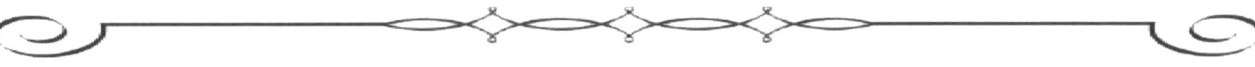

Practicing Presence™ Day 27

Today I practiced being aware of my thought patterns:
_____
_____
_____

Today I practiced identifying the patterns (beliefs) that get in my way:
_____
_____
_____

Today I practiced planting the following positive seeds of thought:
_____
_____
_____

Today I practiced nurturing and supporting myself by:
_____
_____
_____

Today I practiced consciously allowing myself to pause and feel:
_____
_____
_____

Today I focused on power words and images which resulted in:
_____
_____
_____
_____

Remember there is no such thing as a small
act of kindness. Every act creates a ripple with no logical end.
~ Scott Adams

Practicing Presence™ Day 28

Today I practiced being aware of my thought patterns:
_____
_____
_____

Today I practiced identifying the patterns (beliefs) that get in my way:
_____
_____
_____

Today I practiced planting the following positive seeds of thought:
_____
_____
_____

Today I practiced nurturing and supporting myself by:
_____
_____
_____

Today I practiced consciously allowing myself to pause and feel:
_____
_____
_____

Today I focused on power words and images which resulted in:
_____
_____
_____
_____

Notes

Yet it is in this loneliness that the deepest activities begin. It is here that you discover act without motion, labor that is profound repose, vision in obscurity, and, beyond all desire, a fulfillment whose limits extend to infinity.
~ Thomas Merton

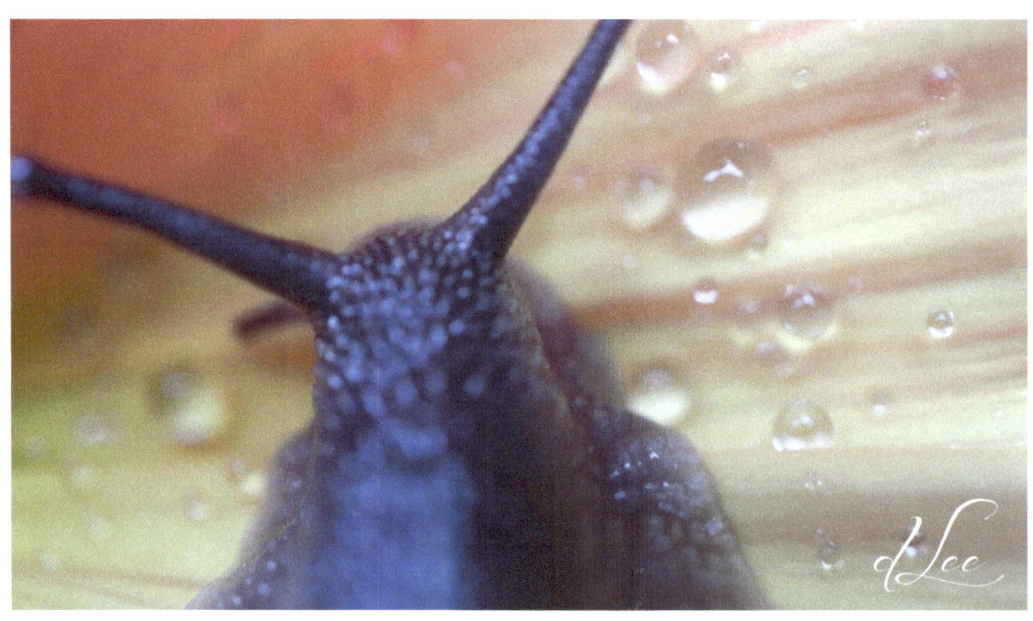

The word "almost" (there) has given many people courage to follow their dream even at the times when it seems quite impossible.
~ Abhilash Katta

Practicing Presence™ Day 29

Today I practiced being aware of my thought patterns:
___
___
___

Today I practiced identifying the patterns (beliefs) that get in my way:
___
___
___

Today I practiced planting the following positive seeds of thought:
___
___
___

Today I practiced nurturing and supporting myself by:
___
___
___

Today I practiced consciously allowing myself to pause and feel:
___
___
___

Today I focused on power words and images which resulted in:
___
___
___
___

Notes

There are two ways of spreading light: to be
the candle or the mirror that reflects it.
~ Edith Wharton

Plant the seed of kindness deep in your inner being and as you nurture it within, watch closely as it opens widely and blooms on the outside of your soul.
~ dLee

Practicing Presence™ Day 30

Today I practiced being aware of my thought patterns:
_____
_____
_____

Today I practiced identifying the patterns (beliefs) that get in my way:
_____
_____
_____

Today I practiced planting the following positive seeds of thought:
_____
_____
_____

Today I practiced nurturing and supporting myself by:
_____
_____
_____

Today I practiced consciously allowing myself to pause and feel:
_____
_____
_____

Today I focused on power words and images which resulted in:
_____
_____
_____
_____

Notes

Flowers always make people better, happier, and more helpful; they are sunshine, food and medicine for the soul.
~ Luther Burbank

Wow!

The time is now to congratulate yourself
on taking the inner journey of
Practicing Presence™ with Inner Kindness!
~ dLee

Practicing Presence™ Day 31

Today I practiced being aware of my thought patterns:
___
___

Today I practiced identifying the patterns (beliefs) that get in my way:
___
___

Today I practiced planting the following positive seeds of thought:
___
___

Today I practiced nurturing and supporting myself by:
___
___

Today I practiced consciously allowing myself to pause and feel:
___
___

Today I focused on power words and images which resulted in:
___
___
___

WORD SCRAMBLES

PAGE 18 KEY - POWER WORD SCRAMBLE

APPRECIATE
AWESOME
BLISS
BUOYANT
CHEERFUL
CONSCIOUS

CONSIDERATE
DELICIOUS
DILIGENT
EFFORTLESS
ELOQUENT
ENTERPRISE

PAGE 62 KEY - HIGH ENERGY WORD SEARCH

G	M	O	P	T	I	M	I	S	T	I	C
W	Y	N	O	M	R	A	H	N	K	U	K
S	P	A	R	K	L	I	N	G	Q	C	J
P	N	I	X	G	N	O	R	T	S	G	K
H	T	T	T	H	A	N	K	F	U	L	A
A	N	H	S	U	O	I	C	I	L	E	D
P	A	R	T	L	U	F	E	C	A	R	G
K	I	I	Z	H	R	E	D	N	O	W	W
V	D	V	H	L	F	A	E	X	E	C	K
M	A	I	N	T	N	A	D	N	U	B	A
S	R	N	B	E	A	U	T	I	F	U	L
M	U	G	J	W	X	L	O	Y	F	G	X

Loving yourself starts with
liking yourself,
which starts with
respecting yourself,
which starts with thinking
of yourself in positive ways.
~ Jerry Corsten

Notes

Inspiration is all around us every day. Be present and accept the colorful abundant invitations from nature, give yourself a gift of being rather than doing.   ~ dLee

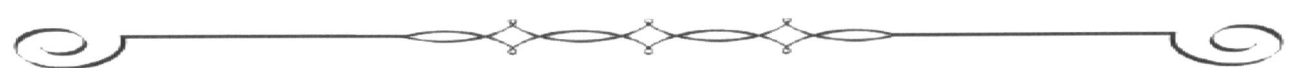

About the Author

dLee is a lifelong high-energy thinker and looks on the bright side of life. She knows that success is about feeling good, taking inspired action and living larger through creative expression. She is an avid photographer with a curious eye for capturing the unique natural images many people will typically just pass by.

Check out dLee's collection of empowering and uplifting images at:

EssenceOfAuthenticPresence.com

www.ingramcontent.com/pod-product-compliance
Lightning Source LLC
Chambersburg PA
CBHW040058160426
43192CB00003B/104